SIERRA CLUB WILDLIFE LIBRARY ELEPHANTS

SIERRA CLUB WILDLIFE LIBRARY

ELEPHANTS

Eric S. Grace

General Editor, R. D. Lawrence

Sierra Club Books for Children
San Francisco

The Sierra Club, founded in 1892 by John Muir, has devoted itself to the study and protection of the earth's scenic and ecological resources – mountains, wetlands, woodlands, wild shores and rivers, deserts and plains. The publishing program of the Sierra Club offers books to the public as a nonprofit educational service in the hope that they may enlarge the public's understanding of the Club's basic concerns. The Sierra Club has some sixty chapters in the United States and in Canada. For information about how you may participate in its programs to preserve wilderness and the quality of life, please address inquiries to Sierra Club, 730 Polk Street, San Francisco, CA 94109.

Text copyright © 1993 by Eric S. Grace
Illustrations copyright © 1993 by Dorothy Siemens

Photographs: © Yann Arthur-Bertrand / Auscape International, 49; © Brian Beck, 3, 5, 32, 37, 44, 46, 47, 51, 56, 57, 59; © John Canalosi / Auscape International 19; © Ralph H. Clevinger / First Light, 25 (middle and bottom), 54; © Gerald and Buff Corsi / Tom Stack and Associates, 9; © Tim Davis / Photo Researchers Inc., 1, 24; © Gregory G. Dimijian / Photo Researchers Inc., 38; © John Downer / Planet Earth Pictures, 20; © Jeanne Drake, 14, 48; © Jean-Paul Ferrero / Auscape International, 62; © Warren Garst / Tom Stack and Associates, 61; © G. C. Kelley / Photo Researchers Inc., 21; © Kenya Wildlife Fund, 7; © Stephen J. Krasemann / DRK Photo, 23; © Jeffrey McNeely / WWF, 31; © F. S. Mitchell / Tom Stack and Associates, 28; © Pat Morrow / First Light, 18; © Peter Pickford / WWF, 35; © Planet Earth Pictures, 34; © Ian Redmond, 1, 6, 33, 55; © Kevin Schafer / Tom Stack and Associates, 10; © Inge Spence / Tom Stack and Associates, 42; © J. D. Taylor, 8; © Belinda Wright / DRK Photo, 25 (top); © Robert L. Zakrison, 40.

First edition

Library of Congress Cataloging-in-Publication Data
Grace, Eric S.
   Elephants / text by Eric S. Grace.
      p.   cm. – (Sierra Club wildlife library)
   Includes index.
   Summary: Describes the physical characteristics of the elephant, how it searches for food and behaves in its natural environment, and how it interacts with people.
   ISBN 0-87156-538-2
   1. Elephants – Juvenile literature. [1. Elephants.] I. Title. II. Series.
QL737.P98G66   1993
599.6'1–dc20   92-32835

Published in Canada by Key Porter Books Limited, Toronto, Ontario
Printed in Hong Kong

10 9 8 7 6 5 4 3 2 1

Contents

Encounters in the Forest

An African elephant can be hard to spot when it stands among trees.

An adult elephant is enormous. You'd think it would be easy to see, wouldn't you? That's what I thought, too, until I visited Africa and almost drove right past an elephant only a few yards from the road. It was standing perfectly still in a clump of tall bushes. Its body was partly hidden, and its shape was broken by shadows. The dull, dusty-colored animal blended into its surroundings and was given away only by the slow flapping of its giant ears. The elephant was completely at home among the scrubby bushes and thorny trees under the tropical sun.

I saw many other elephants during my visit. Some were alone, but most were in groups, moving slowly across the brown and green African landscape. Elephants are powerful, majestic, and intelligent animals. They are also gentle, full of character, and always fascinating to watch. However often I saw elephants, I never lost my sense of pleasure at each encounter or my surprise at their ability to slowly disappear from sight into a group of trees or a dry riverbed.

Elephants can live in many habitats, from open grasslands to thick forests. But today the largest number of elephants is found in Africa's bush country – patches of woodland scattered across grassy plains. On a different continent – among the forests and swamps of India, Sri Lanka, and Thailand – live the smaller Asian elephants, which are now quite rare in the wild.

Elephants are easily the largest living land animals. But despite their size, they can move quietly and unobtrusively, as I discovered while camping in an African woodland.

Early one morning, I was awakened in my tent by the noise of breaking twigs and loud chewing nearby.

I peered out cautiously to find that a small group of elephants had crept up to my campsite while I slept. They now paused for a snack just a short distance away – so close that I could smell their warm elephant scent on the breeze. They waved their trunks back and forth along the branches of the trees, like shoppers pondering a selection of items on a supermarket shelf. After making their choices, they skillfully snapped off sprays of twigs and leaves and swept them casually into their mouths. When they finished munching, my visitors strolled off through the forest with hardly a sound.

An elephant spends about two-thirds of the day feeding.

Lions may prey on unprotected young elephants, or on old and weak elephants.

Although elephants are usually peaceful, they can be dangerous if they feel threatened. Often, but not always, they first signal their annoyance by shaking their head and making loud trumpeting noises. If they are in a group, they move close together and face whatever has disturbed them – perhaps a lion that has come too close or an inquisitive human watching them from a vehicle. The elephants spread their ears wide and twirl their trunks. The largest elephant in the group marches back and forth in front of the others, kicking up dust and working itself into a rage. Finally, this lead elephant coils its trunk up out of the way and begins a lumbering charge – usually enough to scare off any intruder.

A typical day in the life of an elephant consists mostly of eating and walking. From a hilltop at sunrise, I have watched a group of elephants drift slowly from one clump of woodland to another, feeding as they go. A large herd may split into smaller groups throughout the morning. On clear days, when the sun is at its peak and the day is at its hottest, the

elephants gather in a shady spot to rest. Adults usually take a short nap standing up, while tired youngsters lie on their sides to sleep. They continue their journey in the late afternoon; by sunset, the elephants may have traveled anywhere from ten to thirty miles. Late at night or in the early hours of the morning, they stop to sleep again for a few hours before resuming their foraging.

Until the 1960s, few scientific studies were devoted to elephants in the wild, and not much was known about their way of life. European explorers and hunters believed that elephant herds were led by large males, or *bull* elephants. We now know that the herd leader is an older female.

How old do elephants get? How many offspring does a mother elephant have during her lifetime? Do elephants have any natural enemies? How much living space do they need? Years of patient observation have answered questions like these. Bit by bit, the answers have contributed to a picture of a remarkable animal that deserves our greatest respect and care.

When alarmed, an elephant spreads its ears wide and looks toward the source of the noise or smell that has disturbed it.

The First Elephants

The tapir, a large, piglike animal, has a long, flexible nose that looks like an elephant's trunk, only smaller.

In 1900, a group of people traveling on sleds in the desolate northern regions of Asia made an amazing discovery. Sticking out from the frozen ground was part of an animal that had lived there more than 10,000 years earlier. It was a large, hairy, elephantlike creature called a *woolly mammoth*. Although scientists cannot know exactly how the animal died, it may have been knocked down in a landslide that buried it completely beneath layers of ice and frozen soil. Over a period of hundreds of centuries, perhaps after movements in the earth had shifted it, and after warm weather had melted the ice and rains had washed away the soil, a part of the mammoth became visible above the ground.

Like food kept in a freezer, the mammoth was almost perfectly preserved. Its skin and hair were in good condition, and the people who found it even fed some of its flesh to their sled dogs. Inside the mammoth's stomach were the remains of its last meal – grasses and twigs of birch and willow.

The discovery of the frozen mammoth was an exciting glimpse into the past – a glimpse at a relative of the elephant that no human beings had seen alive since the Stone Age. Several more frozen mammoths have since been found in parts of northern Europe, Asia, and North America. The discoveries show that these prehistoric elephants were once common and widespread.

Paleontologists (people who study life-forms that existed long ago) and other scientists have also found the remains of many other extinct elephantlike animals that lived even further back in time. The skin and flesh of these animals have long since rotted away, but their bones and teeth have been preserved as impressions in the rock, or *fossils*. This fossil evidence tells us that there have been about 300 different types, or *species*, of elephants living on earth. Scientists call all these elephant-like animals *proboscideans* (pro-bos-SID-ee-ans), meaning animals with a long snout, or proboscis.

The oldest fossils of a proboscidean found thus far are of a *Moeritherium*, an animal that lived about fifty million years ago. This distant ancestor of today's elephants was about the size of a large pig. It had tiny tusks in both its upper and lower jaws and had a long, rounded snout. It probably spent most of its time wallowing in muddy swamps, eating waterweeds. You might not think this animal looks much like the elephants we know today, but its bones and teeth were similar to those of modern elephants.

Over millions of years, proboscideans slowly developed into larger and larger animals. Their increased size posed a problem, however. To support their large, heavy heads, they had short, thick necks. But a short neck makes it difficult for a tall animal to bend down and reach the ground to feed. As a result, some proboscideans developed longer jaws. Over time, they came to depend more and more on their long snouts to help them gather food. A modern-day animal called a *tapir* has a trunklike snout that it uses in this way. The tapir's bendable snout allows it to grab several plant stems and hold them tightly against its lower jaw while it tugs the plants out of the ground.

By about twenty million years ago, proboscideans looked more like modern elephants. Their bodies were big and bulky, their snouts had lengthened into trunks, and they had large tusks. They lived on every continent except Australia and Antarctica. Because proboscideans lived in a variety of places, with

ELEPHANT ANCESTORS

Long ago, many different types of elephantlike animals lived on earth. Not all of these ancestors of the modern elephant were large, but they had one thing in common. They all had a long snout, or *proboscis*. That is why scientists call them *proboscideans*. The *Moeritherium* (a) was one of the earliest proboscideans. It lived fifty to thirty-five million years ago. The shovel-like lower tusks of the *Platybeledon* (b), which lived twenty-six to seven million years ago, were probably used to scoop plants from swamps. The largest species of extinct proboscidean was *Deinotherium* (c). It lived from seven to two and a half million years ago. The woolly mammoth (d) lived in northern parts of the world. It probably became extinct about 10,000 years ago.

(a)

(b)

(c)

(d)

The hyrax, found mainly in Africa, is the closest living land relative of the elephant.

different climates and different types of plants for food, they developed into a variety of species. Some had four tusks – two in each jaw. Others had wide, flat plates instead of lower tusks, which they probably used like shovels to scoop up plants from the bottoms of swamps. On islands in the Mediterranean Sea lived small prehistoric elephants that looked like our modern species, but were only three to six feet high.

Most prehistoric elephants became extinct more than a million years ago. A few species, however, were still around when early human beings began to spread into North and South America, about 30,000 years ago. The two most common types were the mammoths and the *mastodons*. Mammoths, among the largest of the modern elephant's ancestors, were covered in fur and lived in the cold northern regions of the world. Mastodons resembled the modern elephant more closely than mammoths in size and appearance. Some had four tusks; others had two tusks that grew out of their lower jaw. Great herds of American mastodons once lived in the valley of the Hudson River in what is now New York State. Many of their fossils have been found there. Our Stone Age ancestors hunted mammoths and mastodons for meat and fur and drew pictures of them on the walls of caves.

Today there are only two species of elephants in the world: the African elephant and the Asian elephant. Strangely enough, their closest living relative on land is a small, marmotlike animal called a *hyrax*. Though it doesn't look a bit like an elephant, the hyrax does have hooves and bones that are similar to those of an elephant. The hyrax also has a very long period of pregnancy for such a small animal – nearly eight months. The hyrax and the elephant, together with an animal called the *sea cow*, probably all evolved from the same ancestor, which lived more than sixty million years ago.

HOW CAN YOU TELL AN AFRICAN ELEPHANT FROM AN ASIAN ELEPHANT?

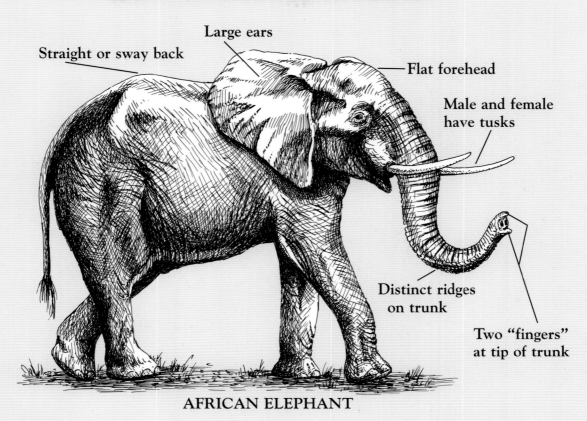

Straight or sway back

Large ears

Flat forehead

Male and female have tusks

Distinct ridges on trunk

Two "fingers" at tip of trunk

AFRICAN ELEPHANT

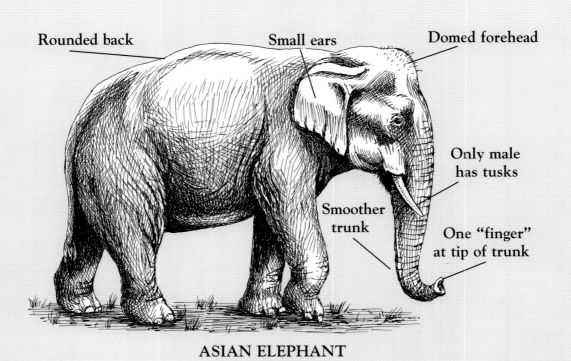

Rounded back

Small ears

Domed forehead

Only male has tusks

Smoother trunk

One "finger" at tip of trunk

ASIAN ELEPHANT

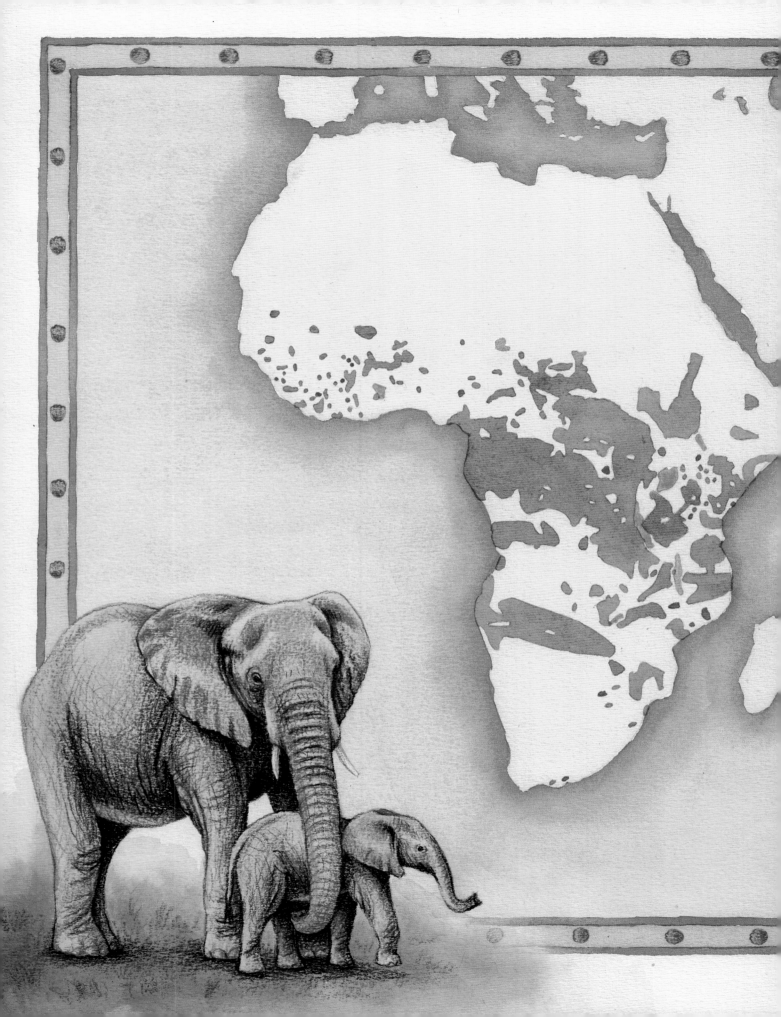

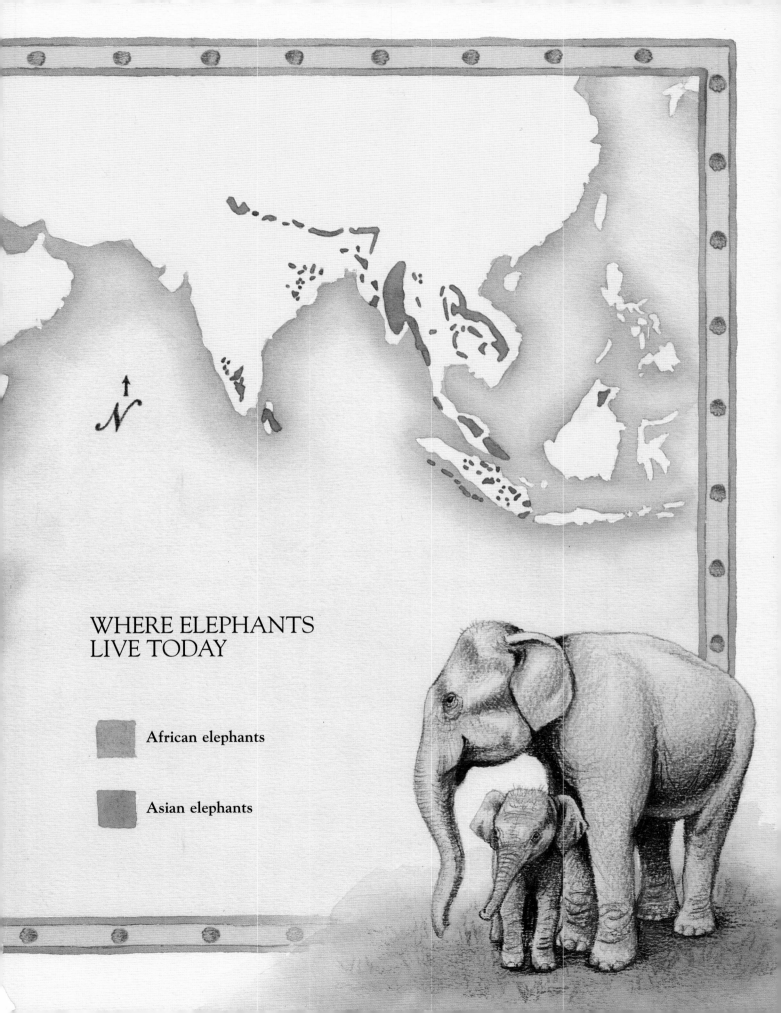

WHERE ELEPHANTS LIVE TODAY

African elephants

Asian elephants

Elephant Anatomy

Elephants can grow to an awesome size. The tallest elephant ever recorded was about thirteen feet high at the shoulder. The heaviest was twelve and a half tons – more than the weight of a loaded, seventy-two-seat school bus. One ear of an African elephant is big enough to cover your bed! You might think such giants would be awkward or clumsy, but in fact elephants are graceful and sensitive animals. To begin to understand the elephant, it is helpful to look closely at the parts of its body. Each part helps the elephant survive – by helping it get food and water, communicate with other elephants, or protect itself from enemies.

TRUNK

An elephant uses its amazing trunk as a combination nose and hand. With its trunk, an elephant can smell, suck up or blow out water and dust, and pick up objects as small as peanuts or as large as tree trunks. An elephant also makes noises with its trunk and uses it to pet or slap other elephants.

The trunk is formed from the elephant's nose and upper lip, which are fused together. It is made up of many muscles that allow it to twist and turn in all directions. Ridges on the underside of the trunk help the elephant get a firm grip on anything it coils its trunk around. One or two "fingers" at the tip of the trunk are used for delicate tasks – just as you might use your thumb and forefinger. The trunk also has short, bristly hairs at its tip that give it a heightened sense of touch.

The two most important jobs of the trunk are breathing and carrying food and water to the elephant's mouth. If its trunk is seriously injured,

An elephant can reach high and low to feed on the leaves of tall trees and on grass or low-growing plants.

18

The elephant uses its trunk as both a hand and a nose.

an elephant may be unable to feed or drink, and it may soon die.

Elephants have a good sense of smell. If you look at the tip of an elephant's trunk, you can see two nostrils. Thanks to its trunk, an elephant can raise its nostrils high above its head to catch the scent of ripe fruit as far away as two or three miles – or lower them to sniff a fallen seed pod on the ground near its feet. With this sensitive organ, an elephant can detect water below the surface of the ground – a vital skill in the dry season, when many rivers and water holes dry up.

A young elephant gives itself a shower.

When elephants gather to bathe at a river or lake, their trunks take on the role of shower hoses. To wash itself, an elephant first sucks water into its trunk and then blows the water out while waving its trunk over its back and sides. Using its suction power in the same way, an elephant can also give itself a dust bath. It frequently does this soon after taking a dip in the water. The dust sticks to the elephant's wet skin, forming a mud pack that helps keep the animal cool and keeps its skin from getting dry, cracked, or burned. The mud pack may also discourage skin parasites such as biting lice or ticks.

Young elephants playing in deep water use their trunks as breathing tubes, or snorkels. It's amusing to watch the small animals gradually wade out until the water covers their heads. Soon all you can see are the tips of their trunks waving, snakelike, above the surface of the river. Their "snorkels" are particularly

useful to the youngsters when the herd must cross a river. A one-year-old could easily become submerged while following its mother through water that barely comes above the adult's belly.

Within their closely knit family groups, elephants frequently greet and touch one another with their trunks. Like good friends holding hands, a pair of elephants may stand with the ends of their trunks hooked together. A mother elephant uses her trunk to give a baby elephant a helping "hand" if the baby stumbles. If an older calf gets to be a nuisance, a mother may also use her trunk to smack the mischief maker.

With all these jobs to do, an elephant's six-foot tube of solid muscle sometimes grows tired and feels heavy. Perhaps this is why an elephant can sometimes be seen standing at rest with its trunk draped limply over one tusk.

The trunk may serve as a sort of snorkel through which the elephant breathes when almost submerged in water.

21

HEAD, EYES, AND EARS

Inside their huge heads, elephants have bigger brains than do any other land animal. There is some evidence that elephants have good memories. In a time of drought, for example, they seem to be able to find their way back to sources of water that they may not have visited for a long time. They are certainly intelligent and able to learn quickly.

The heavy weight of an elephant's massive head and tusks is lightened by many air spaces inside the bone of the skull. Because of the size of its head, an elephant's eyes appear small. Close up, you can see that each eye is screened by a set of five-inch-long eyelashes. In bright light, an elephant's eyesight is not very keen; also, its short neck does not allow it to turn its head to look behind. Elephants therefore rely more on their senses of smell and hearing than on sight.

The ears of an adult African elephant are enormous. Each ear is about six feet from top to bottom and nearly five feet across. Asian elephants have smaller ears. One reason for this difference may be that African elephants live mainly in hot, open bush country rather than in shady forests, and their large ears help them stay cool. Here's how the cooling process works: Each ear contains many blood vessels close to the surface of the thin skin. The blood vessels carry warm blood from the rest of the body. When an elephant is hot, it slowly flaps its ears like fans. The fanning cools the blood in the ears by as much as ten degrees Fahrenheit, and the cooler blood then circulates back into the body. Flapping its ears also helps the elephant keep away annoying flies.

When an elephant is angry or feels threatened, it spreads its ears wide and faces whatever has alarmed it. The added ten-foot ear span makes the elephant look even bigger than usual.

With its ears spread wide, an advancing elephant appears to be even bigger than it really is.

This elephant is using its tusks to dig up earth, which it eats for the mineral and salt content.

TUSKS AND TEETH

An elephant's tusks are actually large teeth. They grow out of the elephant's upper jaw and continue to grow slowly throughout the animal's life. The tusks are made of a hard material called *ivory*. Both male and female African elephants have tusks. Most female Asian elephants do not. In some parts of their range – for example, in Sri Lanka – most male Asian elephants do not have tusks either. Elsewhere, including in much of southern and central India, most Asian male elephants do have tusks. The longest elephant tusk on record – eleven and a half feet – belonged to a bull African elephant. The heaviest recorded single tusk, also taken from an African elephant, weighed an incredible 237 pounds.

Elephants use their tusks as digging tools to get at water or salt in the ground or to uproot small trees so they can feed on the roots and top branches. Tusks also serve as chisels for peeling the bark off tree trunks and as levers for moving fallen trees. Elephants occasionally use their tusks as weapons when they are fighting one another or protecting themselves and their offspring from large predators such as lions or tigers.

Like people, elephants may be either "right-handed" or "left-handed," and favor using one tusk over the other. As a result, the tusk that is used more becomes worn and polished at the tip and is usually slightly shorter than the other tusk.

Baby elephants grow tiny tusks that are about two inches long. These first tusks drop out, and the permanent ones grow in, usually before the elephant's first birthday. An elephant can be recognized by its tusks, which have their own distinct shape, size, and color. Some pairs of tusks spread apart at the tips. Others grow together and may even touch. Some are straight, some are curved, and some are broken at the end. The part that you can see is only about two-thirds of the total length of the tusk. The other one-third is firmly rooted in the bone of the upper jaw.

The tusks are the elephant's *incisors*, or cutting teeth. An elephant also has four *molars*, or grinding teeth – one on each side of the upper jaw and one on each side of the lower jaw. The molars have large ridges of enamel on their chewing surfaces. When an elephant chews its food, it moves its lower jaw backward and forward, rubbing the ridges over one another like files. Because an elephant grinds and chews tons of vegetation each month, the ridges on the molars eventually wear down. As this happens, the molars are replaced by new ones that grow behind the old. An elephant grows six complete sets of molars during

An elephant's tusks may be short and thick, long and slender, straight or curved.

WHAT IS INSIDE AN ELEPHANT?

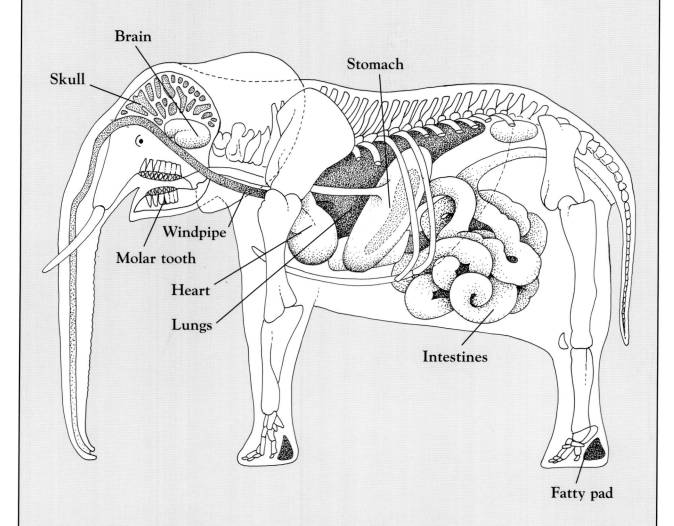

Brain

Skull

Stomach

Windpipe

Molar tooth

Heart

Lungs

Intestines

Fatty pad

An elephant's body has a number of special features because it is so large and heavy. The elephant's skull, parts of which may be six inches thick, makes up as much as a quarter of its total body weight. It would be even heavier if the skull were solid bone, but it is not. Many small air spaces make the inside of the skull look something like a sponge.

To help cushion its weight when it walks, the sole of the elephant's foot has a thick fatty pad. The pad is thicker at the back of the foot, so the elephant almost walks on tiptoe!

its lifetime. The new molars slowly move forward in the elephant's mouth, as if they were on a conveyor belt.

The sixth and last set of molars is huge. Each tooth is about a foot long and weighs about ten pounds. This final set comes into use when an elephant is in its early forties, and must last the animal for the rest of its life. After these molars wear smooth, the elephant cannot chew its food properly. An old elephant slowly loses condition as it gets less and less nourishment, and it rarely survives much past sixty years of age. An elephant is one of the few wild animals that can generally live out its full life span and die of old age. Scientists can tell how old an elephant was at death by studying the condition of its teeth.

LEGS AND FEET

The elephant's stocky body is supported on four pillarlike legs. Sturdy leg bones and wide, flat feet hold the weight evenly. A walking elephant moves both legs on the same side of its body at the same time. Walking this way gives the animal a gentle, side-to-side, rolling motion.

Between its toes and on the soles of its feet, an elephant has thick pads of soft, springy flesh. These pads absorb the shock of the elephant's steps. When the elephant places its weight on them, they swell under the pressure like inflatable cushions. When the elephant lifts its foot, the pads shrink again. The soles of an elephant's feet are sensitive, and the animal must pick its way carefully and cautiously over rough ground. An elephant cannot jump, but it can run in short bursts at speeds of up to twenty miles an hour when it is angry or frightened.

SKIN

The wrinkled skin that covers an elephant's body can be up to an inch thick in places. This is why some people call elephants *pachyderms* (PACK-i-durms), from the Greek words meaning "thick-skinned." Unlike most mammals, an elephant does not have a layer of fat under its skin or a covering of thick fur. Both fat and fur would be disadvantages to an elephant, because they would cause the animal to become easily overheated. Even without fat and fur, an elephant regularly wallows in mud or bathes in water to help keep itself cool.

Elephants cover themselves with a layer of mud to help keep cool.

A PROBLEM OF SIZE

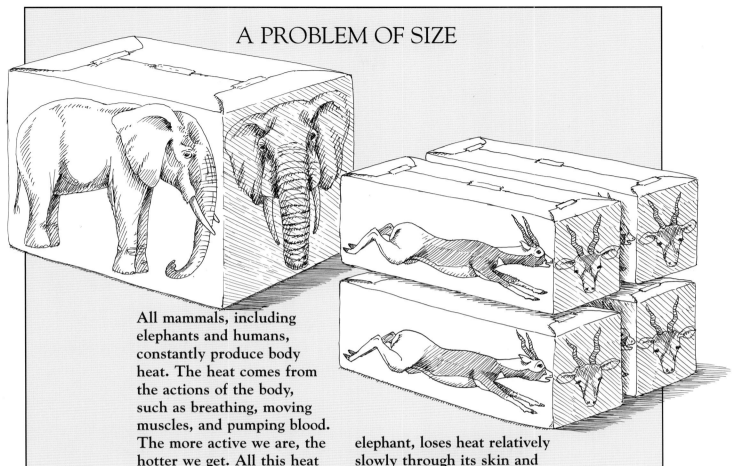

All mammals, including elephants and humans, constantly produce body heat. The heat comes from the actions of the body, such as breathing, moving muscles, and pumping blood. The more active we are, the hotter we get. All this heat is eventually lost from the body through the skin. If it weren't, we would soon get overheated.

How quickly an animal can lose heat is related to the size of its body. Relative to its size, a big animal has a smaller area of skin than a small animal does. You can see this relationship in the drawing. It takes a lot less wrapping paper (or skin) to wrap one big box than it does to wrap four smaller boxes that together fill the same amount of space as the big one.

Because of the relationship of volume to surface area, a big animal, such as an elephant, loses heat relatively slowly through its skin and has a problem staying cool. On the other hand, a small animal, such as a mouse, loses heat rapidly through its skin and has a problem staying warm. To balance this, big animals generally produce less body heat and maintain a lower body temperature than small animals.

A scientist once calculated that if a cow produced body heat as rapidly as a mouse does, its skin temperature would soon rise above the boiling point! And if a mouse produced body heat the way a cow does, it would need to grow fur eight inches thick to keep warm!

Family Life

In order to find out how elephants live in the wild, scientists have had to get to know them as individuals. They have done this by watching groups of elephants carefully over several years. This involves following the elephants to see where they go and what they do. It also involves keeping records of when babies are born and when animals die or move out of the area.

Such careful observation depends on the ability of researchers to tell one elephant in a herd from another. To help identify individual elephants, researchers first take photographs of each elephant's head. The photographs are labeled and placed in an album, which can be used later to keep track of elephants seen in the study area. Like people, no two elephants look exactly alike. One might have very straight tusks; another, a jagged tear in one ear; a third, a large, bony forehead. With a little practice, anyone can learn to recognize the different elephants by matching them up with their photos in the album.

The following description of life within a group of elephants is based on several studies carried out in the bush country of East Africa. However, most of the observations probably hold true for elephants living in other parts of Africa and in Asia as well.

LIFE IN THE HERD

A group of ten elephants stands in the shade at the edge of a forest, resting during the midday heat. It is a typical family group, made up of female elephants, called *cows*, and their calves. All the elephants in this group are related to one another. The oldest female is the leader, or *matriarch*, of the group. This particular matriarch has four offspring, including an adult

daughter who has a newborn calf of her own. The other adult female in the group is the matriarch's sister. She is the mother of a twelve-year-old bull and two younger calves.

Family groups such as this are the basis of elephant society. A group can be as small as three or four, or as large as twenty-five or more. Female elephants usually spend their lives with the group into which they were born. The size of the group increases when female calves grow up and have calves of their own. A cow elephant may have her first calf when she is about twelve years old, and may continue breeding until she is in her fifties. A large family group may include four generations, with elephants ranging in age from a newborn calf to a matriarch of sixty years or more. Cows generally do not become matriarchs until they are forty or fifty years old. They hold the position until they die. If a group grows very large, one or two females and their calves may split off to form a new family group of their own a few miles away.

Scientists studying elephants in the field tell one from another by noting the pattern of notches and veins in the ears and the distinctive length and curve of the tusks.

31

A typical family group is made up of adult females with calves of different ages.

Unlike their sisters, male calves leave the family group shortly after they reach puberty, at about thirteen years of age. During adolescence, the young bull elephants become more and more boisterous. They spar with other calves and even with adults. As they become bigger and stronger, their mock battles grow more serious. Eventually, the older females in the family may chase a quarrelsome young bull away or threaten him whenever he comes close to them or their younger calves. For a time, perhaps as long as two or three years, the rejected youngster trails along behind his family group. Gradually, he becomes more independent until finally he wanders off alone or joins a small group of other bulls.

The members of a family group always walk, eat, sleep, and play close together, rarely straying more than fifty yards from the matriarch. During the course of a day, as a group of elephants moves in search of food and drink, its path often crosses those of other groups living in the same large area. These over-lapping groups are often connected by family ties. The matriarch of one group might be the cousin, daughter, or sister of the matriarch of a neighboring group.

From time to time, several family groups may join together to form big herds of one hundred elephants or more. These large gatherings are most likely to occur in times of plenty – for example, when there has been heavy rain and the grasses and plants that the elephants feed on are abundant. At such times, there is enough food and water to sustain a large number of elephants in a small area. It is an awesome sight to watch so many elephants pass by like a grand procession. Giant matriarchs flap their ears and smell the air with upraised trunks. Tiny infants trot quickly to keep up, while playful adolescents trumpet and run ahead. As they move along, the elephants help themselves to clumps of grass or to seed pods that have fallen from trees. Within the large herd, an experienced observer can still pick out the separate family groups, each of which has its own identity. A big herd may stay together for several days, but eventually it breaks up again into the basic family groups.

Both male and female elephants are usually peaceful and easygoing, sharing their resources with other elephants. They settle most disputes with displays of head shaking and trumpeting. Smaller animals move out of the way of larger ones. Only rarely do elephants have fights that cause serious

Large herds of elephants such as this are made up of several family groups.

Two young bulls test their strength against each other.

injuries. Throughout their lives, however, bulls often play-fight with other bulls of similar age and size. They lock tusks, twine their trunks like arm wrestlers, and twist and lunge at each other. Torn ears and bleeding wounds sometimes result from the slash and jab of an opponent's tusk, especially if two bulls are evenly matched in strength and the fight lasts a long time. When the contest is over and a winner decided, the bulls are tolerant of each other once again. Such combats help each elephant know its place within the population of bulls.

Adult bulls do not seem to become permanently attached to any particular family group or to other individuals. Groups of bulls rarely stay together for long. Usually, the only time mature bulls are found with groups of cows is when one or more cows in the group are ready for mating. This can occur at any time of year.

When a bull encounters a group of cows, the cows greet him by reaching out their trunks and touching his mouth. The bull sniffs the cows and can tell from their smell if it is the right time for mating. If it is, the bull will stay with the group for several days, mating with any females that are ready. Several other bulls may also join the group, and more than one bull may mate with the same cow. Usually, however, the most dominant bull – often the largest – threatens the others and keeps them at a distance. All the elephants become excitable at mating time, and often the herd is loud with trumpeting and growling.

After mating, bulls leave the female group and go off on their own again. Meanwhile, in the cows that have mated, the fertilized egg begins its long period of development. Nearly two years go by from the time of mating until the birth of the baby elephant. This *gestation period*, lasting from twenty to twenty-two months, is the longest of any known animal.

HOW DO ELEPHANTS COMMUNICATE?

Most of elephants' communication with one another cannot be heard by humans. This amazing fact was discovered several years ago when scientists recorded elephants and played back their recordings at high speed. In the speeded-up versions, the scientists discovered that elephants often make rumbling noises that are pitched below the range of sound that people can normally hear. These low-frequency noises, probably made in the elephant's throat, can travel for miles through bush country. They let elephants stay in contact when they are widely separated and out of sight of one another.

In addition to rumbling, elephants also squeak, trumpet, gurgle, and chirp to one another. A trumpeting screech, unmistakable even to human ears, lets every animal within earshot know that the trumpeter is angry, threatened, or afraid.

When they are within sight of one another, elephants can also communicate through "body language." A shaking head seems to mean "Don't bother me." Ears spread wide may mean "Watch out!" A bull elephant striding quickly with his head high tells others that he is on the lookout for a mate. When a member of the herd raises her trunk in the air, the others can see that she has detected a far-off scent – it could be food, danger, or other elephants.

Smell and touch are also used for communication when elephants are close together. An elephant places the tip of its trunk into another's mouth to greet it or to reassure it in a moment of stress. Elephants often feel and stroke each other with their trunks. Using their keen sense of smell, elephants can find out if another elephant is sick, ready to mate, or about to give birth.

BIRTH OF AN ELEPHANT

About a half hour before sunrise, the herd begins to move. The elephants slip quietly from the shelter of their resting place and make their way slowly across the grassy plain. Grandmothers and mothers lead the way, with the younger elephants close behind. As the herd moves on toward the woodland where it will spend the morning feeding, one elephant trails the rest. She is a young cow, about fourteen years old, who will soon give birth to her first calf.

Unlike most other animals, whose bellies grow noticeably bigger when they are carrying young, a pregnant elephant shows little or no sign of swelling. Only her behavior reveals that something is about to happen. The mother-to-be moves about restlessly for a few minutes, as if uncertain what to do. Spotting a thick clump of trees and bushes to one side of the path, she walks over to it and is soon out of sight of the herd. Now about twenty yards away, other members of the herd become aware that she is gone or hear her calls, and they stand still as if waiting for something to happen.

In the privacy of her hiding place, the young female stands quiet and still. Suddenly, a dark bulge appears between her back legs as the birth begins. Within seconds, the baby elephant has slipped out from its mother's body and dropped onto the ground, still enclosed in a thin-walled bag of fluid called the *birth sac*.

Almost before the mother has had time to turn and touch the newborn baby gently with her front foot, two older females from the herd join her. They stand close beside the mother and calf, softly feeling them with their trunks and helping the struggling baby escape from its birth sac. Just fifteen minutes or so after being born, with a little help from mother's

This baby elephant is only a few days old.

foot held carefully underneath it and her trunk steadying its wobbly legs, the baby elephant stands up.

Baby elephants look like miniature adults, except that they have no tusks and often are covered with hair. Most of the hair disappears as the calf grows older. At birth, an elephant weighs about 250 pounds and stands just under three feet at the shoulder.

Although elephants normally give birth to a single calf, rare cases of twins have been recorded. Even more rarely do both twins survive, possibly because the mother does not produce enough milk

*A mother elephant keeps close
watch on her youngster.*

to raise two large youngsters. A cow may produce up to ten calves in her lifetime.

The younger cows in the herd appear to be fascinated by the new addition to their family. They jostle one another and investigate with their trunks, trying to get as close as possible to the baby. In the middle of the crowd, the anxious mother stands firmly beside her offspring. Two or three times, her baby falls over and she helps it back onto its feet. The excitement soon dies down, and most of the other elephants move off to feed. After an hour or so, when the baby has gained strength, the mother leads her still wobbly firstborn slowly out from the trees into the open space.

Within a few hours of birth, the baby elephant discovers its mother's nipples. Unlike horses and cows, which have udders between their back legs, a female elephant has two breasts between her front legs. The baby flaps its ears, shakes its head, and reaches up to drink. It bends its trunk out of the way and suckles hungrily with its mouth.

Elephant calves may be born at any time of year. There are usually more births after a season of heavy rainfall, when plants grow tall and green and there is more food for the elephants. During long periods of drought, there may be no calves born in a herd for as long as two or three years. When the rains return, the elephants begin to reproduce again. Often, all the adult females in a particular group give birth to their calves within a few days or weeks of one another.

GROWING UP

Mother elephants care for their young longer than any animals except human beings and some whales. For the first few months of its life, the calf is rarely

Older calves may be looked after by any adults in the group.

more than a few steps away from its mother. The mother watches her baby closely and follows it protectively when it begins to explore the world around it. As the group moves on its daily journeys, she helps the small calf scramble up riverbanks or clamber over fallen branches, giving it support with her trunk or foot. The mother sometimes steers her youngster ahead of her by holding onto the baby's tail with her trunk, like someone walking a pet dog on a leash. Other elephants in the group also lend a helping trunk when needed, and the baby soon gets to know all the members of its family by their touch and smell.

Each growing calf develops a unique personality. Some like to stay safely beside their mothers, while others are bold and active. As with all baby animals, a young elephant's curiosity and enthusiasm sometimes get it into trouble. Whenever it feels lost or gets stuck or is playfully shoved by its older sisters or brothers, the frightened calf lets out a loud squeak. This sound brings the adults rushing over to see what is wrong. Some timid babies complain over every stumble, however, and their mothers soon learn to leave small problems to the care of the young cows in the group.

A small calf often appears puzzled about what to do with its trunk. At first, the trunk seems to get in the way rather than being of any real use. The baby swings the trunk back and forth, and round and round, like a wiggly rubber toy. After a few weeks, the calf begins to pick up small objects with the tip of its trunk, but it doesn't yet have the skill and coordination to put the objects where it wants them. The calf tries bending its trunk into a U-shape and balancing twigs in the curve. It may grasp a leaf and break it off, but then drop the leaf or put it on top of its head instead of into its mouth. When exhausted, the calf may let its trunk dangle limply in front of it and then step on the end and trip. A tired baby elephant often sticks the end of its trunk into its mouth and sucks, like a human baby sucking its thumb. It takes about a year for the young elephant to learn to use its trunk properly and keep it under control.

At a year old, the calf is still small enough to stand underneath its mother's belly. It is always close to its mother at this age. It continues to nurse and constantly seeks her protection from the sun, from too-boisterous playmates, and from possible attack by lions or tigers. Now, however, it spends more time with other elephants in the group. An adult cow will protect and care for any calf and will readily adopt a baby whose own mother has died, especially if the cow does not have a calf of her own. Partly grown calves mingle freely within their family group, and it is not always possible for a human observer to know exactly which of the older calves belong to which cows.

Calves spend much of their time playing together. A favorite game is for a calf to try to climb onto an elephant that is lying down. An older calf will sometimes try to get a younger calf to climb on it by lying down beside the younger one. When the smaller calf has its front legs on top and is trying to haul the rest of its body up the steep slope of its playmate's back, the older calf stands up and sends the infant sliding to the ground. Calves spar and tussle with each other, butt their heads together, and push and shove. They chase one another with squeals of excitement, the pursuers trying to grab the tails of the calves in front of them with their trunks.

Calves play many games together.

Although a calf may begin eating some plant food a few months after its birth, it continues to drink its mother's milk until it is about two years old. After that, calves are able to survive on plants alone, but most still suckle occasionally for a few years more. When her calf is two years old, the mother may mate again. Because pregnancy lasts nearly two years, there is roughly a four-year age difference between offspring.

Between the ages of four and ten, young elephants grow, learn about their environment, and develop bonds with other elephants in the family group. They learn where to look for food and water and what places are dangerous. Older female calves may begin to help look after a newborn baby sister or brother, learning some of the skills they will need when they become mothers themselves.

MATURITY

By their early teens, male and female calves begin to take on the different roles of adult bulls and cows. Young cows reach puberty between the ages of eight and twelve years. They are then able to mate and become pregnant, even though they are only two-thirds the size of a full-grown cow. Teenage bulls leave the care of their mother's family group. However, they may not mate with cows until they are thirty years old or older and able to compete with other adult bulls.

Adult bull elephants periodically go through a strange and little understood condition known as *musth* (pronounced MUST). During these periods, the bulls become aggressive and unpredictable. They spend less time eating and more time searching for cows ready to mate. When a bull is in musth, glands on both sides of its head swell and produce a liquid

Mature bull elephants live either alone or, occasionally, in the company of one or two other bulls.

that streams down the bull's face. At the same time, there is an increase in the amounts of male sex hormones in the bull's blood. A bull usually comes into musth once a year, and the condition may last for three months or longer. In fights over females, a bull in musth usually wins. If both rivals are in musth, the fight may become very violent. Such fights can last for several hours and can result in one bull being badly injured or even killed by its opponent.

FACING DANGER

The things most likely to be life-threatening change as an elephant grows older. Small calves that are still suckling can starve to death during dry years, when many plants wither and turn brown, because their mothers may be unable to produce enough milk for them. The first few months of life are also the time when an elephant is most likely to be killed by a predator. Young elephant calves are occasionally killed by lions or hyenas in Africa and by tigers in Asia.

The next time of danger for male calves is when they reach puberty and leave their family group. Without the protection of the herd and the matriarch's knowledge of where to find food and water, young bulls may starve or have fatal accidents. Elephants wandering in unfamiliar territory have been known to slip and fall into pits or wells or to tumble down steep slopes. Elephants gouging out the bases of old, rotted trees with their tusks have been killed by the trees falling on them. And a young bull that unwisely annoys an older bull may be pursued and killed in a fight.

From young adulthood through the middle years, elephants rarely die of natural causes. Like all wild animals, they experience their share of diseases, such as pneumonia and anthrax. They also suffer from parasites, such as worms and ticks. However, a robust elephant can usually survive most diseases and parasites.

The final, unavoidable threat comes when an elephant's last set of teeth wears smooth in old age. This usually happens when it is in its mid fifties. Without the benefit of a proper diet, the elephant's body cannot fight off disease so easily. As for many humans, a heart attack or stroke may be the final blow that ends the weakened elephant's life.

ONE OF THE LAST GREAT TUSKERS

At the time of his death in January 1974, the wild African elephant named Ahmed was being tracked day and night by a team of armed soldiers. Ahmed was thought to have the largest tusks of any elephant then alive, and the soldiers were there to protect him from hunters.

Ahmed was born about the year 1919, probably near the area in northern Kenya where he died fifty-five years later. The name Ahmed is Arabic and means "praised." Ahmed certainly was praised by all those lucky enough to see him. His tusks, each about ten feet long and weighing about 150 pounds, actually bumped on the ground as he walked. He appeared in many books, magazine articles, and films during the early 1970s. He became a legend and was known around the world. Hunters after trophies were among the people who heard about him.

Thousands of people wrote to the East African Wildlife Society to express their concern for the elephant's safety. As a result, the president of Kenya passed a decree to protect Ahmed and sent the soldiers to follow him.

Ahmed died of natural causes deep within his forest home. The authorities decided to preserve his skin, bones, and tusks and display them in a museum. A road was cut through the trees to reach his carcass, and the body was guarded for four days while the skin was carefully removed. In the end, however, the skin became badly decomposed and could not be saved. Today, a fiberglass model of Ahmed (see photo) stands outside the National Museum of Kenya in Nairobi. It is a reminder of the splendor of Africa's wildlife as it used to be. Unfortunately, it is a splendor that has been lost.

Today, fewer and fewer wild elephants die of old age. By far the greatest threat to their life comes from people. Thousands of elephants are killed each year by poachers, who illegally sell the elephants' tusks to ivory dealers. In the parks and protected areas of Zimbabwe and in some other countries in southern Africa, scientists say there are more elephants than the land can support. In these areas, park rangers and licensed hunters shoot hundreds of elephants each year. As farms and villages encroach on elephant country, many elephants are killed by people protecting their property. You can read more about the impact of humankind on elephants later in this book.

An old elephant may die of starvation, disease, or accident. Some are killed by predators.

The Search for Food

An elephant may use both its trunk and its tusks to strip the bark off a tree.

To get enough food to fuel its huge body, an adult elephant must spend more than two-thirds of its time eating. During a twenty-four-hour period, an elephant will consume between 200 and 350 pounds of vegetation, depending on its size.

The types of plants an elephant eats depend on what time of year it is and where the elephant lives. Researchers in East Africa have found that elephants are not fussy eaters but instead have wide tastes. They eat bits and pieces of several hundred different species of plants during the year.

On the open grasslands, or *savannahs*, grasses are the most common food during the rainy season. Elephants seem to prefer the tall, tough grasses that other animals do not eat. After sniffing and touching a clump of grass with the tip of its trunk, an elephant wraps its trunk tightly around a bunch of stems. With a firm tug, and perhaps a kick or two at the base of the stems to loosen them, the elephant pulls up the grass by the roots. A particularly careful eater may then knock the plants against one knee to shake off the dirt before lifting the meal to its mouth.

In wooded areas or when dry weather has turned grasses brown, elephants feed on the leaves, twigs, bark, roots, and fruits of shrubs and trees. Like people, they seem to prefer some foods to others. They may walk a mile or two following the scent of a favorite fruit, completely ignoring some of the common plants around them. Prized foods include figs, wild bananas, black plums, and wild coffee berries. In dense forests, elephants can sniff out the leaves of low-growing wild ginger and sweet aloe, which may be hidden beneath taller plants. Herds that live in forests high on a mountainside enjoy the wild celery, bamboo, and raspberries that grow in these cooler areas. In swamps,

48

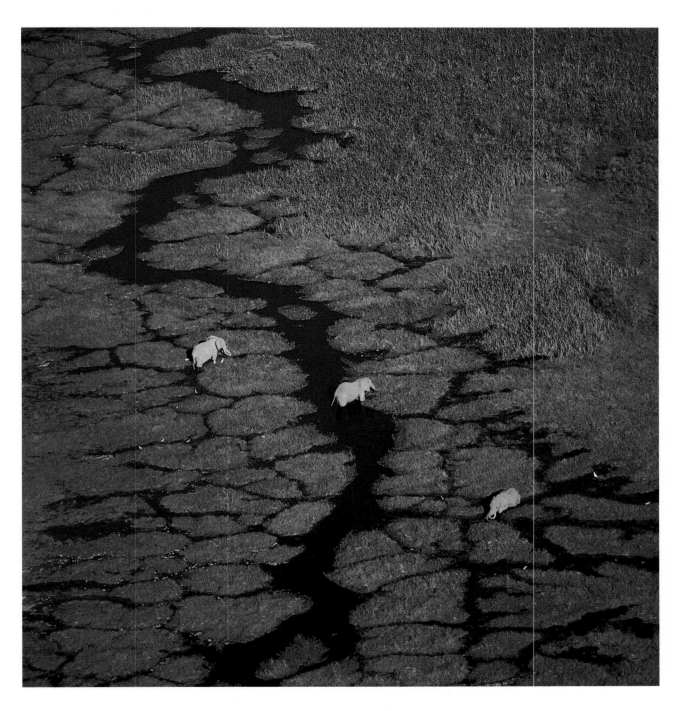

Elephants that live in swampy areas may spend a lot of time swimming or wading to reach their favorite plants.

reeds and water plants are their main foods. During the dry season, when many small water holes and streams disappear, elephants search out plants with thick, juicy leaves or fleshy fruit. The large, succulent leaves of *Sansevieria* are an important source of moisture for elephants in some parts of Africa. Elephants chew on the leaves to extract the juices and then spit out the tough fibers that remain.

Baby elephants learn what to eat by watching adults. Often a baby will reach its trunk into its mother's mouth while she is eating and pull out a bit of her half-chewed meal. By the age of nine months, calves spend nearly half their time picking at bits of plants, but they still depend on their mothers' milk as much as younger calves do. If a calf is not well fed during its first year, its health is likely to be poorer than normal for the rest of its life.

Almost everything an elephant eats and drinks is obtained with the help of its trunk. Bending and swaying in search of food, an elephant's trunk may sweep back and forth across the ground, curl upward to probe a bush, or reach high above the elephant's head into the branches of a tree. Without moving its body, an elephant can be feeding twenty feet above the ground one minute and gathering leftovers from the forest floor the next.

Elephants also use their tusks to help them get food. They stab their tusks into trees to remove strips of bark or to reach the juicy pith that lies just underneath the bark. Tusks are also useful tools for digging out buried roots and bulbs.

In their never-ending search for food and drink, a herd of elephants may walk as far as thirty miles in twenty-four hours during the dry season. In wet weather, when plants are growing all around, the elephants may stay in one small area. The routes that elephants take in their daily wanderings depend as much on

water as on food. If plenty of juicy plants are available, elephants may go several days without drinking. However, they still prefer to be close to water, where they can bathe as well as drink. A large lake or river may become the group's home base for a time. The elephants may return to it each evening after a day spent feeding some distance away. Because of their size, elephants can wade across shallow rivers or lakes; they are also able to swim in deeper water.

While they are at their watering places, elephants often take the opportunity to wallow in the cool mud or perhaps take a dust bath. You can tell where an elephant has been most recently by the color of the dust or mud on its skin. Rust-colored elephants have been crossing the dusty red soils common in many parts of the tropics. Gray elephants have been wallowing in silty river mud. Darker-coloured elephants have been to a mud pool in an area with black volcanic soil.

A group of elephants on the move often walks along well-used routes, following one another in single file.

51

A DAY IN THE LIFE OF AN AFRICAN ELEPHANT FAMILY GROUP

During a typical day and night, a group of elephants may walk about ten to thirty miles. Elephants spend about nineteen hours out of every twenty-four feeding.

Midnight to 4:00 A.M.: Feed and rest

4:00 A.M. to 6:00 A.M.: Rest

6:00 P.M. to midnight: Feed and walk

6:00 A.M. to noon: Feed and walk

Noon to 3:00 P.M.: Rest

3:00 P.M. to 4:00 P.M.:
Join neighboring group

4:00 P.M. to 6:00 P.M.:
Drink, bathe, feed beside
lake with other elephants

Male elephant
joins group

A group of elephants has a dust bath.

Along with food and water, animals also need salt and other minerals in order to survive. Elephants usually get their salt from plants; the plants, in turn, obtain salt from the soil. But in areas where heavy rains wash salt deep down into the ground, plants contain little salt. In such places, elephants and other plant eaters must eat or lick small bits of soil and rock that contain salt. Places where many salty rocks are found at the surface of the ground are called *salt licks*. Large numbers of animals visit these spots. Elephants break off small chunks of rock with their tusks and chew the chunks as you might chew hard candy. One large elephant may chew and swallow as much as fifty pounds of rock during a visit to a salt lick.

THE AMAZING UNDERGROUND ELEPHANTS

On the slopes of a huge, extinct volcano in East Africa, elephants gouging out rocks for salt have produced an astonishing curiosity. Over the course of thousands of years, generations of elephants have dug out huge caves with their tusks.

The remarkable cave-digging elephants were discovered in the 1980s by a wildlife biologist named Ian Redmond. While observing elephants in the area, he was amazed to see them walking into caves. He carefully followed a group of about twenty elephants as they slowly felt their way into a deep, pitch-black cavern. Then, using a flashlight, he saw the elephants scraping the underground rock walls with their tusks. Later, using special lighting, he took pictures of the elephants tusking the walls of the cave.

The sight of elephants chiseling out hollows in the side of a cliff to get salt is not unusual. Elephant-made cuttings up to fourteen feet high can be seen in cliff faces in several parts of Africa. Once these hollows have gone a few feet into the cliff, they leave rocky overhangs that usually soon crumble and fall. The collapsing roof prevents a cave from being dug very far into the cliff. What is unusual about the area studied by Ian Redmond is that it has a layer of tough volcanic rock above the salty rock. The volcanic rock makes a strong ceiling that stays intact even when the softer rock below it is mined. As a result, the largest cave extends more than 160 yards into the mountain and in some places is as wide 100 yards. It's big enough to hold an entire herd of elephants!

That elephants alone can dig such a large cave may seem incredible. But remember that every elephant can dig out a bucketful or more of rock in a night. And elephants have lived in this area for about five million years.

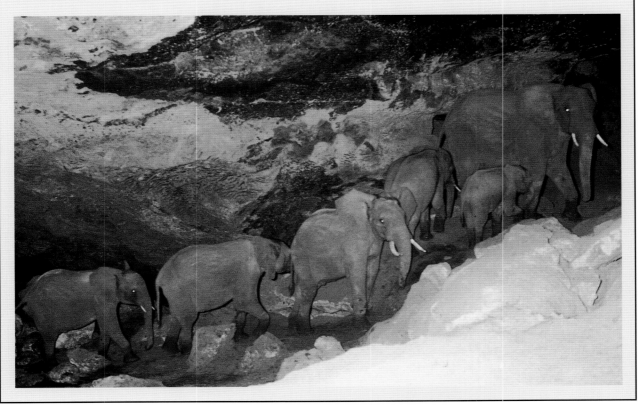

Elephants and Their Environment

White egrets follow elephants in order to feed on the insects that the elephants disturb.

Imagine that suddenly, overnight, all the elephants in a large region of Africa mysteriously vanished. Within a short time, you would notice many changes in the grasslands and forests. Some animals and plants might become more common. Many others would become rare or disappear. Nearly everything, from small beetles to giant trees, would be affected in some way. For example, elephants regularly feed on bushes. This keeps the bushes from spreading and choking out grasses and small plants. This, in turn, helps all the animals that feed on the grasses and small plants. It also helps the predators that feed on those animals. By eating bushes, elephants help preserve the large variety of living things in their environment.

Because they are such big animals, elephants have a large effect on the landscape around them. When they push over trees in the forest, more sunlight comes in. This allows sun-loving plants to grow on the forest floor. Without elephants, some areas would develop into dense, dark forests, with only a few types of plants growing beneath the trees. The sun-loving plants make up a particular kind of habitat in the forest, providing shelter and food for ground-living animals. Elephants also leave behind broken branches and fallen twigs and fruits that are later eaten by smaller forest animals.

Areas of Africa in which many elephants live often have a patchwork of open woodlands mixed with grasslands and scattered bush. In the woodlands live browsing animals such as impalas, gazelles, and giraffes. On the grasslands live grazing animals such as zebras and wildebeests. Where most or all of the elephant population has been killed, thick bush and forest usually take over. As this happens, fewer and fewer types of animals can live in the area.

While elephants keep some fast-growing bushes and trees from spreading, they help other plants grow over a wider area. Some plant seeds hitch a ride by lodging between an elephant's toes. Others are consumed by the elephant and carried in its stomach. Several hours afterward, the seeds pass through the elephant's body and fall to the ground inside its dung. By this time, the elephant may have traveled several miles, with the result that the seeds of the plants have spread over long distances. Elephants are the only animals large enough to eat the coconut-size fruits of certain palm trees, which usually grow near water. The seeds of the palm trees are inside the fruits. Lines of palm trees sometimes mark the routes taken by elephants between the palm-fringed rivers and their other feeding grounds.

The impact of elephants on their surroundings depends partly on how many elephants there are in an area. It also depends on the weather. During dry periods, elephants (as well as other animals) tend to

Zebras and giraffes are among the many animals that live where elephants are plentiful on the African plains.

57

gather in large numbers around the few remaining pools of water. Herds of elephants can soon turn a shallow pool into a mud wallow, unsuitable for drinking. On the other hand, elephants can provide new supplies of water for themselves and other animals by digging out water holes with their tusks, trunks, and feet.

Along streams and rivers, elephants may unintentionally change the course of the water by trampling out gullies or digging into riverbanks. When heavy rains return and the rivers swell, water surges into these elephant-made channels. Often the water floods out of the channels and washes away soil from the land.

In Africa, the dry season often brings fires. These fires also help prevent open grasslands from developing into bush country. The flames quickly burn off dead grass stems and destroy dry, scrubby bushes and small saplings. Ashes from the fire fertilize the ground and encourage new grasses to spring up as soon as it rains. Without such fires, there would be far fewer open plains with their huge numbers of grazing animals.

Large trees are usually not killed by fires because their bark is resistant to burning. However, when elephants strip off the bark to eat, the trees are no longer protected. Elephants also help fires spread far into forests by pushing down trees and leaving open spaces. When the plants that grow up in these open spaces dry out, they can easily catch fire and carry the flames along the forest floor.

You can see from these examples that the relationships among animals, plants, and weather can be very complicated. In many parts of Africa today, the activities of people are being added to this tangled web. For example, people have been cutting forests to establish farms and villages. This has forced elephants

out of many places where they used to live. Crowded into smaller areas with less food, the elephants damage and kill trees faster than the trees can grow back.

The soft wood of the baobab tree is a source of vitamins and minerals for African elephants.

The loss of trees in parts of Africa has affected more animals than the ones that feed or nest in them. For example, a leopard typically hunts its prey by jumping on it from the branches of a tree. Where there are fewer trees, there are fewer leopards. A shortage of trees also makes life harder for gazelles, which gather in the shade of trees to find shelter from the midday sun. Elephants are more adaptable than many other animal species. Some elephant populations survive on the slopes of mountains, and others find food and water on the edges of deserts. But most elephants look for shelter under trees during the hottest part of the day. Just as forests are shaped and sustained by elephants and other animals, so the animals are sustained by forests.

Elephants and People

Since the time of the prehistoric mammoths and mastodons, people have trapped and hunted elephants for their meat, skin, and ivory tusks. A big bull elephant with long tusks is a frightening animal to face with only a spear, but one dead elephant would provide a huge amount of food and other goods for a hunter's family.

By about 4,000 years ago, there was already an important trade in elephant ivory, which people used for carvings, tools, jewelry, and building materials. During the time of the Roman Empire, which began 2,000 years ago, there was an even greater demand for ivory. One Roman emperor built a stable out of ivory for his horse. The Romans killed so many elephants that they were largely responsible for the elephants' disappearance from northern Africa.

At the same time as people began killing elephants for their tusks, they also learned to trap and tame live elephants. The elephants were caught in pits or with lassos, or were driven into fenced enclosures. Sometimes baby elephants were captured after all the adults in their herd had been killed. Captured wild elephants can be tamed quite easily and taught to carry out various tasks. People have used elephants to haul timber, carry soldiers and weapons into battle, and perform in parades and circuses. Both African and Asian elephants can be tamed, but Asian elephants are more commonly used for training today.

The number of elephants killed for ivory grew during the 1800s, when European hunters and explorers invaded Africa. Until the 1950s, however, elephants still survived in large numbers over much of Africa. Huge herds followed their age-old routes in search of food and water, and there were many old elephants with massive tusks.

Over the past forty years, several factors have led to a massive slaughter of African elephants. Not only is there still a big demand for ivory in some parts of the world, but people are paying more and more to get it. Killing elephants and selling ivory are now against the law in many countries, but the high price of ivory encourages poachers to risk their lives killing elephants illegally. Motor vehicles, and even helicopters and airplanes, can take hunters with high-powered guns into remote areas where there are no authorities to stop them.

Asian elephants are still used in lumber camps to move and carry logs.

61

The survival of young elephants like this one depends largely on humankind.

The elephants that survive illegal hunting have ever smaller areas in which to live. Many forests where they once fed have been cleared. Elephant paths have been blocked by fences, fields, and villages. Elephants that try to cross these barriers are often killed by the local people.

Confined to small areas in protected parks or driven into regions that are less suitable for them, the elephants themselves soon begin to destroy their own habitat. When elephants kill trees by pushing them over or stripping off their bark, concerned people argue that there are too many elephants in one place. The presence of too many elephants, in turn, threatens the survival of other animals and plants. As a result, some elephants are deliberately shot to solve the problem of "overpopulation." In 1990, an estimated 600,000 elephants remained in Africa – less than half the number living there in 1970. In Asia, the pressure from human population growth has reduced the number of wild elephants to no more than 50,000.

The sad outcome of these developments can be seen in many parts of Africa today. Old elephants with big tusks are now extremely rare. Many of the old matriarchs, on which family groups depend, have died. Elephant families are now led by younger, less experienced animals who may not know where to go and how to survive when food and water are scarce. Through human greed and inaction, elephants may disappear from the wild during your lifetime. These magnificent animals' only chance of survival is for people to act now to protect their habitats and save their lives.

INDEX

Numbers in italics refer to photographs.